MW00508394

Air Fryer Cookbook: Delicious Recipes

Explore New Recipes in this Book

By

Caroline Taylor

Table of content

Air Grilled Cheese Roll-Ups

(Ready in about 10 minutes | Servings 3)

Per serving:

395 Calories; 26.4g Fat; 21.1g Carbs; 16.9g Protein; 2.5g Sugars

Ingredients

6 slices bread

2 tablespoons butter 6 slices Colby cheese

A pinch of ground black pepper

Directions

Flatten the bread slices to 1/4-inch thickness using a rolling pin. Spread the melted butter on top of each slice of bread.

Place a cheese slice on top of each slice of bread; sprinkle with black pepper and roll them up tightly.

Bake the cheese roll-ups at 390 degrees F for about 8 minutes. Bon appétit!

Authentic Prosciutto Bruschetta

(Ready in about 10 minutes | Servings 3)

Per serving:

269 Calories; 12.4g Fat; 20.5g Carbs; 18.9g Protein; 3.7g Sugars

Ingredients

3 slices sourdough bread 1/2 cup marinara sauce 3 slices mozzarella 6 slices prosciutto 6 fresh basil leaves

Directions

Using a rolling pin, flatten the bread slightly.

Spread the marinara sauce on top of each slice of bread, then, top with mozzarella and prosciutto.

Now, bake your bruschetta at 360 degrees F for about 8 minutes until the cheese is melted and golden.

Garnish with basil leaves and serve. Bon appétit!

Baked Tortilla Chips

(Ready in about 15 minutes | Servings 3)

Per serving:

167 Calories; 6.1g Fat; 26.4g Carbs; 3.2g Protein; 0.5g Sugars

Ingredients

1/2 (12-ounce) package corn tortillas 1 tablespoon canola oil

1/2 teaspoon chili powder

1 teaspoon salt

Directions

Cut the tortillas into small rounds using a cookie cutter.

Brush the rounds with canola oil. Sprinkle them with chili powder and salt.

Transfer to the lightly greased Air Fryer basket and bake at 360 degrees F for 5 minutes, shaking the basket halfway through. Bake until the chips are crisp, working in batches.

Serve with salsa or guacamole. Enjoy!

Basic Air Fryer Granola

(Ready in about 45 minutes | Servings 12)

Per serving:

103 Calories; 6.8g Fat; 8.8g Carbs; 3.1g Protein; 3.1g Sugars

Ingredients

1/2 cup rolled oats

1 cup walnuts, chopped

3 tablespoons sunflower seeds 3 tablespoons pumpkin seeds 1 teaspoon coarse sea salt

2 tablespoons honey

Directions

Thoroughly combine all Ingredients and spread the mixture onto the Air Fryer trays. Spritz with nonstick cooking spray.

Bake at 230 degrees F for 25 minutes; rotate the trays and bake 10 to 15 minutes more.

This granola can be kept in an airtight container for up to 2 weeks. Enjoy!

Beef and Wild Rice Casserole

(Ready in about 50 minutes | Servings 3)

Per serving:

444 Calories; 13.1g Fat; 49.6g Carbs; 34.3g Protein; 4.7g Sugars

14

Ingredients

3 cups beef stock

1 cup wild rice, rinsed well 1 tablespoon olive oil

1/2 pound steak, cut into strips 1 carrot, chopped

1 medium-sized leek, chopped

2 garlic cloves, minced 1 chili pepper, minced

Kosher salt and ground black pepper, to your liking

Directions

Place beef stock and rice in a saucepan over medium-high heat.

Cover and bring it to a boil. Reduce the heat and let it simmer about 40 minutes. Drain the excess liquid and reserve.

Heat the olive oil in a heavy skillet over moderate heat. Cook the steak until no longer pink; place in the lightly greased baking pan.

Add carrot, leek, garlic, chili pepper, salt, and black pepper. Stir in the reserved wild rice. Stir to combine well.

Cook in the preheated Air Fryer at 360 degrees for 9 to 10 minutes. Serve immediately and enjoy!

Cheese and Bacon Crescent Ring

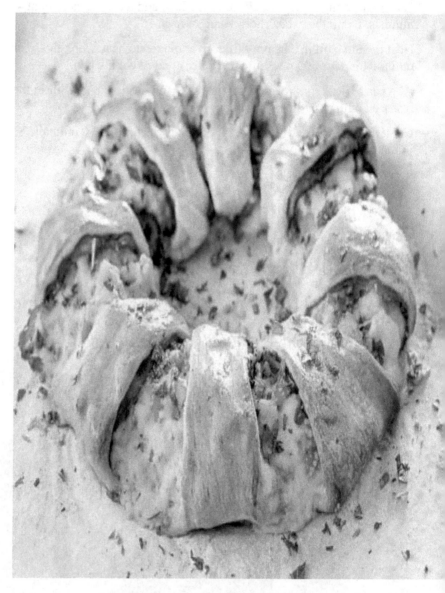

(Ready in about 25 minutes | Servings 4)

Per serving:

506 Calories; 30.8g Fat; 33.6g Carbs; 21.7g Protein; 6.9g Sugars

Ingredients

1 (8-ounce) can crescent dough sheet

1 ½ cups Monterey Jack cheese, shredded 4 slices bacon, cut chopped

4 tablespoons tomato sauce 1 teaspoon dried oregano

Directions

Unroll the crescent dough sheet and separate into 8 triangles. Arrange the triangles on a piece of parchment paper; place the triangles in the ring so it should look like the sun.

Place the shredded Monterey Jack cheese, bacon, and tomato sauce on the half of each triangle, at the center of the ring. Sprinkle with oregano.

Bring each triangle up over the filling. Press the overlapping dough to flatten. Transfer the parchment paper with the crescent ring to the Air Fryer basket.

Bake at 355 degrees F for 20 minutes or until the ring is golden brown. Bon appétit!

Ciabatta Bread Pudding with Walnuts

(Ready in about 45 minutes | Servings 4)

Per serving:

454 Calories; 18.2g Fat; 56.7g Carbs; 18.3g Protein; 25.1g Sugars

Ingredients

4 cups ciabatta bread cubes 2 eggs, slightly beaten

1 cup milk

2 tablespoons butter

4 tablespoons honey

1 teaspoon vanilla extract 1/2 teaspoon ground cloves

1/2 teaspoon ground cinnamon A pinch of salt

A pinch of grated nutmeg 1/3 cup walnuts, chopped

Directions

Place the ciabatta bread cubes in a lightly greased baking dish. In a mixing bowl, thoroughly combine the eggs, milk, butter, honey, vanilla, ground cloves, cinnamon, salt, and nutmeg.

Pour the custard over the bread cubes. Scatter the chopped walnuts over the top of your bread pudding.

Let stand for 30 minutes, occasionally pressing with a wide spatula to submerge.

Cook in the preheated Air Fryer at 370 degrees F degrees for 7 minutes; check to ensure even cooking and cook an additional 5 to 6 minutes. Bon appétit!

Cinnamon Breakfast Muffins

(Ready in about 20 minutes | Servings 4)

Per serving:

302 Calories; 17.1g Fat; 27.7g Carbs; 8.3g Protein; 3.3g Sugars

Ingredients

1 cup all-purpose flour

1 teaspoon baking powder 1 tablespoon brown sugar 2 eggs

1 teaspoon cinnamon powder 1 teaspoon vanilla paste

1/4 cup milk

4 tablespoons butter, melted

Directions

Start by preheating your Air Fryer to 330 degrees F. Now, spritz the silicone muffin tins with cooking spray.

Thoroughly combine all Ingredients in a mixing dish. Fill the muffin cups with batter.

Cook in the preheated Air Fryer approximately 13 minutes. Check with a toothpick; when the toothpick comes out clean, your muffins are done.

Place on a rack to cool slightly before removing from the muffin tins. Enjoy!

Classic Air Fryer Cornbread

(Ready in about 30 minutes | Servings 4)

Per serving:

455 Calories; 23.9g Fat; 46.1g Carbs; 13.9g Protein; 4.7g Sugars

Ingredients

3/4 cup cornmeal 1 cup flour

2 teaspoons baking powder

1/2 tablespoon brown sugar 1/2 teaspoon salt

5 tablespoons butter, melted

3 eggs, beaten

1 cup full-fat milk

Directions

Start by preheating your Air Fryer to 370 degrees F. Then, spritz a baking pan with cooking oil.

In a mixing bowl, combine the flour, cornmeal, baking powder, brown sugar, and salt. In a separate bowl, mix the butter, eggs, and milk.

Pour the egg mixture into the dry cornmeal mixture; mix to combine well.

Pour the batter into the baking pan; cover with aluminum foil and poke tiny little holes all over the foil. Now, bake for 15 minutes.

Remove the foil and bake for 10 minutes more. Transfer to a wire rack to cool slightly before cutting and serving. Bon appétit!

Classic Italian Arancini

(Ready in about 35 minutes | Servings 2)

Per serving:

348 Calories; 7.5g Fat; 52.2g Carbs; 15.8g Protein; 2.4g Sugars

Ingredients

1 ½ cups chicken broth 1/2 cup white rice

2 tablespoons parmesan cheese, grated

Sea salt and cracked black pepper, to your liking 2 eggs

1 cup fresh bread crumbs

1/2 teaspoon oregano 1 teaspoon basil

Directions

Bring the chicken broth to a boil in a saucepan over medium-high heat. Stir in the rice and reduce the heat to simmer; cook about 20 minutes. Drain the rice and allow it to cool completely.

Add the parmesan, salt, and black pepper. Shape the mixture into bite-sized balls.

In a shallow bowl, beat the eggs; in another shallow bowl, mix bread crumbs with oregano and basil.

Dip each rice ball into the beaten eggs, then, roll in the breadcrumb mixture, gently pressing to adhere.

Bake in the preheated Air Fryer at 350 degrees F for 10 to 12 minutes, flipping them halfway through the cooking time. Bon appétit!

Crème Brûlée French Toast

(Ready in about 10 minutes | Servings 2)

Per serving:

407 Calories; 18.8g Fat; 51.7g Carbs; 8.3g Protein; 32.2g Sugars

Ingredients

4 slices bread, about 1-inch thick 2 tablespoons butter, softened

1 teaspoon ground cinnamon

2 ounces brown sugar

1/2 teaspoon vanilla paste A pinch of sea salt

2 ounces Neufchâtel cheese, softened

Directions

In a mixing dish, combine the butter, cinnamon, brown sugar, vanilla, and salt. Spread the cinnamon butter on both sides of the bread slices.

Arrange in the cooking basket. Cook at 390 degrees F for 2 minutes; turn over and cook an additional 2 minutes.

Serve with softened Neufchâtel cheese on individual plates. Bon appétit!

Delicious Turkey Sammies

(Ready in about 50 minutes | Servings 4)

Per serving:

452 Calories; 24.8g Fat; 22.9g Carbs; 38.5g Protein; 9.1g Sugars

Ingredients

1/2 pound turkey tenderloins 1 tablespoon olive oil

Salt and ground black pepper, to your liking

4 slices bread

1/4 cup tomato paste 1/4 cup pesto sauce

1 yellow onion, thinly sliced

1 cup mozzarella cheese, shredded

Directions

Brush the turkey tenderloins with olive oil. Season with salt and black pepper.

Cook the turkey tenderloins at 350 degrees F for 30 minutes, flipping them over halfway through. Let them rest for 5 to 9 minutes before slicing.

Cut the turkey tenderloins into thin slices. Make your sandwiches with bread, tomato paste, pesto, and onion. Place the turkey slices on top. Add the cheese and place the sandwiches in the Air Fryer basket.

Then, preheat your Air Fryer to 390 degrees F. Bake for 7 minutes or until cheese is melted. Serve immediately.

Double Cheese Risotto Balls with Arrabbiata Sauce

(Ready in about 35 minutes | Servings 3)

Per serving:

505 Calories; 21.4g Fat; 60g Carbs; 13.9g Protein; 4.8g Sugars

Ingredients

1 cup Arborio rice 2 tablespoons butter

2 ounces Provolone cheese, grated

2 ounces Asiago cheese, grated 1 egg, whisked

1/3 cup seasoned breadcrumbs, passed through a sieve

1 tablespoon olive oil 1/4 cup leeks, chopped

9 ounces canned San Marzano tomatoes

1 teaspoon red pepper flakes, crushed

2 tablespoons fresh basil leaves, roughly chopped Sea salt and freshly cracked black pepper, to taste

Directions

Bring 3 cups of water to a boil in a saucepan over medium-high heat. Stir in the rice and reduce the heat to simmer; cook for about 20 minutes.

Fluff your rice in a mixing bowl; stir in the butter and cheese. Salt and pepper to taste; shape the mixture into equal balls.

Beat the egg in a shallow bowl; in another shallow bowl, place the seasoned breadcrumbs.

Dip each rice ball into the beaten egg, then, roll in the seasoned breadcrumbs, gently pressing to adhere.

Bake the rice balls in the preheated Air Fryer at 350 degrees F for about 10 minutes, shaking the basket halfway through the cooking time to ensure even cooking.

Meanwhile, heat the olive oil in a saucepan over a moderate flame. Once hot, sauté the leeks until just tender and fragrant.

Now, add in the tomatoes and spices and let it simmer for about 25 minutes, breaking your tomatoes with a spatula. Serve the warm risotto balls with Arrabbiata sauce for dipping.

Bon appétit!

Favorite Cheese Biscuits

(Ready in about 30 minutes | Servings 4)

Per serving:

462 Calories; 25.8g Fat; 39.1g Carbs; 17.6g Protein; 2.1g Sugars

Ingredients

1 ½ cups all-purpose flour

1/3 cup butter, room temperature 1 teaspoon baking powder

1 teaspoon baking soda

1/2 cup buttermilk 2 eggs, beaten

1 cup Swiss cheese, shredded

Directions

In a mixing bowl, thoroughly combine the flour and butter. Gradually stir in the remaining Ingredients.

Divide the mixture into 12 balls.

Bake in the preheated Air Fryer at 360 degrees F for 15 minutes. Work in two batches.

Serve at room temperature. Bon appétit!

Favorite Spinach Cheese Pie

(Ready in about 30 minutes | Servings 4)

Per serving:

521 Calories; 33.9g Fat; 36.1g Carbs; 17.9g Protein; 5.2g Sugars

Ingredients

1 (16-ounce) refrigerated rolled pie crusts 4 eggs, beaten

1/2 cup buttermilk

1/2 teaspoon salt

1/2 teaspoon garlic powder 1/4 teaspoon cayenne pepper

2 cups spinach, torn into pieces 1 cup Swiss cheese, shredded

2 tablespoons scallions, chopped

Directions

Unroll the pie crust and press it into a cake pan, crimping the top edges if desired.

In a mixing dish, whisk together the eggs, buttermilk, salt, garlic, powder, and cayenne pepper.

Add the spinach, 1/2 of Swiss cheese, and scallions into the pie crust; pour the egg mixture over the top. Sprinkle the remaining 1/2 cup of Swiss cheese on top of the egg mixture.

Bake in the preheated Air Fryer at 350 degrees F for 10 minutes. Rotate the cake pan and bake an additional 10 minutes.

Transfer to a wire rack to cool for 5 to 10 minutes. Serve warm.

Greek-Style Pizza with Spinach and Feta

(Ready in about 20 minutes | Servings 2)

Per serving:

502 Calories; 29.5g Fat; 53.6g Carbs; 14.8g Protein; 17.3g Sugars

Ingredients

2 ounces frozen chopped spinach Coarse sea salt, to taste

2 personal pizza crusts

1 tablespoon olive oil 1/4 cup tomato sauce

2 tablespoons fresh basil, roughly chopped

1/2 teaspoon dried oregano 1/2 feta cheese, crumbled

Directions

Add the frozen spinach to the saucepan and cook until all the liquid has evaporated, about 6 minutes. Season with sea salt to taste.

Preheat the Air Fryer to 395 degrees F.

Unroll the pizza dough on the Air Fryer baking tray; brush with olive oil.

Spread the tomato sauce over the pizza crust. Add the sautéed spinach, basil, and oregano. Sprinkle the feta cheese, covering the pizza crust to the edges.

Cook for 10 minutes, rotating your pizza halfway through the cooking time. Repeat with another pizza and serve warm.

Hibachi-Style Fried Rice

(Ready in about 30 minutes | Servings 2)

Per serving:

428 Calories; 13.4g Fat; 58.9g Carbs; 14.4g Protein; 4.7g Sugars

Ingredients

1 ¾ cups leftover jasmine rice 2 teaspoons butter, melted

Sea salt and freshly ground black pepper, to your liking

2 eggs, beaten

2 scallions, white and green parts separated, chopped 1 cup snow peas

1 tablespoon Shoyu sauce 1 tablespoon sake

2 tablespoons Kewpie Japanese mayonnaise

Directions

Thoroughly combine the rice, butter, salt, and pepper in a baking dish.

Cook at 340 degrees F about 13 minutes, stirring halfway through the cooking time.

Pour the eggs over the rice and continue to cook about 5 minutes. Next, add the scallions and snow peas and stir to combine. Continue to cook 2 to 3 minutes longer or until everything is heated through.

Meanwhile, make the sauce by whisking the Shoyu sauce, sake, and Japanese mayonnaise in a mixing bowl.

Divide the fried rice between individual bowls and serve with the prepared sauce. Enjoy!

Honey Raisin French Toast

(Ready in about 5 minutes | Servings 2)

Per serving:

492 Calories; 24g Fat; 57.1g Carbs; 13.2g Protein; 38.7g Sugars

Ingredients

2 eggs

1/4 cup full-fat milk

1/4 teaspoon ground cloves 1/2 teaspoon ground cinnamon 4 tablespoons honey

2 tablespoons coconut oil, melted 4 slices sweet raisin bread

Directions

Thoroughly combine the eggs, mink, ground cloves, cinnamon, honey and coconut oil. Spread the mixture on both sides of the bread slices.

Arrange the bread slices in the cooking basket and cook them at 390 degrees F for 2 minutes; flip and cook on the other side for 2 to 3 minutes more.

Serve with some extra honey if desired. Bon appétit!

Italian Panettone Bread Pudding

(Ready in about 45 minutes | Servings 3)

Per serving:

279 Calories; 8.7g Fat; 37.9g Carbs; 8.9g Protein; 23.1g Sugars

Ingredients

4 slices of panettone bread, crusts trimmed, bread cut into 1-inch cubes 4 tablespoons dried cranberries

2 tablespoons amaretto liqueur

1 cup coconut milk

1/2 cup whipping cream 2 eggs

1 tablespoon agave syrup 1/2 vanilla extract

1/2 teaspoon ground cloves

1/2 teaspoon ground cinnamon

Directions

Place the panettone bread cubes in a lightly greased baking dish. Scatter the dried cranberry over the top. In a mixing bowl, thoroughly combine the remaining Ingredients.

Pour the custard over the bread cubes. Let it stand for 30 minutes, occasionally pressing with a wide spatula to submerge.

Cook in the preheated Air Fryer at 370 degrees F degrees for 7 minutes; check to ensure even cooking and cook an additional 5 to 6 minutes. Bon appétit!

Italian-Style Fried Polenta Slices

(Ready in about 35 minutes | Servings 3)

Per serving:

451 Calories; 4.4g Fat; 91g Carbs; 11.2g Protein; 0g Sugars

Ingredients

9 ounces pre-cooked polenta roll 1 teaspoon sesame oil

2 ounces prosciutto, chopped

1 teaspoon Italian seasoning blend

Directions

Cut the pre-cooked polenta roll into nine equal slices. Brush them with sesame oil on all sides. Then, transfer the polenta slices to the lightly oiled Air Fryer cooking basket.

Cook the polenta slices at 395 degrees F for about 30 minutes; then, top them with chopped prosciutto and Italian seasoning blend.

Continue to cook for another 5 minutes until cooked through. Serve with marinara sauce, if desired. Bon appétit!

Japanese Chicken and Rice Salad

(Ready in about 45 minutes + chilling time | Servings 4)

Per serving:

387 Calories; 4.7g Fat; 63.9g Carbs; 22.4g Protein; 3.9g Sugars

Ingredients

1 pound chicken tenderloins

2 tablespoons shallots, chopped 1 garlic clove, minced

1 red bell pepper, chopped 1 ½ cups brown rice

1 cup baby spinach

1/2 cup snow peas

2 tablespoons soy sauce

1 teaspoon yellow mustard 1 tablespoon rice vinegar

1 tablespoon liquid from pickled ginger 1 teaspoon agave syrup

2 tablespoons black sesame seeds, to serve 1/4 cup Mandarin orange segments

Directions

Start by preheating your Air Fryer to 380 degrees F. Then, add the chicken tenderloins to the baking pan and cook until it starts to get crisp or about 6 minutes.

Add the shallots, garlic, and bell pepper. Cook for 6 minutes more. Wait for the chicken mixture to cool down completely and transfer to a salad bowl.

Bring 3 cups of water and 1 teaspoon of salt to a boil in a saucepan over medium-high heat. Stir in the rice and reduce the heat to simmer; cook about 20 minutes.

Let your rice sit in the covered saucepan for another 10 minutes. Drain the rice and allow it to cool completely.

Stir the cold rice into the salad bowl; add the baby spinach and snow peas. In a small mixing dish, whisk the soy sauce, mustard, rice vinegar, liquid from pickled ginger, and agave syrup.

Dress the salad and stir well to combine. Garnish with black sesame seeds and Mandarin orange. Enjoy!

Last Minute German Franzbrötchen

(Ready in about 15 minutes | Servings 6)

Per serving:

157 Calories; 2.4g Fat; 30g Carbs; 3.1g Protein; 18.6g Sugars

Ingredients

6 slices white bread

1 tablespoon butter, melted 1/4 cup brown sugar

1 tablespoon ground cinnamon Glaze:

1/2 cup icing sugar

1/2 teaspoon vanilla paste 1 tablespoon milk

Directions

Flatten the bread slices to 1/4-inch thickness using a rolling pin. In a small mixing bowl, thoroughly combine the butter, brown sugar and ground cinnamon.

Spread the butter mixture on top of each slice of bread; roll them up.

Bake the rolls at 350 degrees F for 10 minutes, flipping them halfway through the cooking time.

Meanwhile, whisk the icing sugar, vanilla paste and milk until everything is well incorporated. Drizzle the glaze over the top of the slightly cooled rolls.

Let the glaze set before serving. Bon appétit!

Mediterranean Monkey Bread

(Ready in about 20 minutes | Servings 6)

Per serving:

427 Calories; 25.4g Fat; 38.1g Carbs; 11.6g Protein; 6.5g Sugars

Ingredients

1 (16-ounce) can refrigerated buttermilk biscuits 3 tablespoons olive oil

1 cup Provolone cheese, grated

1/4 cup black olives, pitted and chopped 4 tablespoons basil pesto

1/4 cup pine nuts, chopped

1 tablespoon Mediterranean herb mix

Directions

Separate your dough into the biscuits and cut each of them in half; roll them into balls. Dip each ball into the olive oil and begin layering in a nonstick Bundt pan.

Cover the bottom of the pan with one layer of dough balls.

Prepare the coating mixtures. In a shallow bowl, place the provolone cheese and olives, add the basil pesto to a second bowl and add the pine nuts to a third bowl.

Roll the dough balls in the coating mixtures; then, arrange them in the Bundt pan so the various coatings are alternated. Top with Mediterranean herb mix

Cook the monkey bread in the Air Fryer at 320 degrees for 13 to 16 minutes. Bon appétit!

Mexican-Style Brown Rice Casserole

(Ready in about 50 minutes | Servings 4)

Per serving:

433 Calories; 7.4g Fat; 79.6g Carbs; 12.1g Protein; 2.8g Sugars

Ingredients

1 tablespoon olive oil 1 shallot, chopped

2 cloves garlic, minced

1 habanero pepper, minced 2 cups brown rice

3 cups chicken broth

1 cup water

2 ripe tomatoes, pureed

Sea salt and ground black pepper, to taste 1/2 teaspoon dried Mexican oregano

1 teaspoon red pepper flakes

1 cup Mexican Cotija cheese, crumbled

Directions

In a nonstick skillet, heat the olive oil over a moderate flame. Once hot, cook the shallot, garlic, and habanero pepper until tender and fragrant; reserve.

Heat the brown rice, vegetable broth and water in a pot over high heat. Bring it to a boil; turn the stove down to simmer and cook for 35 minutes.

Grease a baking pan with nonstick cooking spray.

Spoon the cooked rice into the baking pan. Add the sautéed mixture. Spoon the tomato puree over the sautéed mixture. Sprinkle with salt, black pepper, oregano, and red pepper.

Cook in the preheated Air Fryer at 380 degrees F for 8 minutes. Top with the Cotija cheese and bake for 5 minutes longer or until cheese is melted. Enjoy!

Mexican-Style Bubble Loaf

(Ready in about 20 minutes | Servings 4)

Per serving:

382 Calories; 17.5g Fat; 50.8g Carbs; 7.1g Protein; 6g Sugars

Ingredients

1 (16-ounce) can flaky buttermilk biscuits 4 tablespoons olive oil, melted

1/2 cup Manchego cheese, grated

1/2 teaspoon granulated garlic

1 tablespoon fresh cilantro, chopped 1/2 teaspoon Mexican oregano

1 teaspoon chili pepper flakes

Kosher salt and ground black pepper, to taste

Directions

Open a can of biscuits and cut each biscuit into quarters. Brush each piece of biscuit with the olive oil and begin layering in a lightly greased Bundt pan.

Cover the bottom of the pan with one layer of biscuits.

Next, top the first layer with half of the cheese, spices and granulated garlic. Repeat for another layer.

Finish with a third layer of dough.

Cook your bubble loaf in the Air Fryer at 330 degrees for about 15 minutes until the cheese is bubbly. Bon appétit!

New York-Style Pizza

(Ready in about 15 minutes | Servings 4)

Per serving:

308 Calories; 4.1g Fat; 25.7g Carbs; 42.7g Protein; 6.1g Sugars

Ingredients

1 pizza dough

1 cup tomato sauce

14 ounces mozzarella cheese, freshly grated 2 ounces parmesan, freshly grated

Directions

Stretch your dough on a pizza peel lightly dusted with flour. Spread with a layer of tomato sauce.

Top with cheese. Place on the baking tray.

Bake in the preheated Air Fryer at 395 degrees F for 5 minutes. Rotate the baking tray and bake for a further 5 minutes. Serve immediately.

Paella-Style Spanish Rice

(Ready in about 35 minutes | Servings 2)

Per serving:

546 Calories; 12.4g Fat; 90.7g Carbs; 17.6g Protein; 4.5g Sugars

Ingredients

2 cups water

1 cup white rice, rinsed and drained 1 cube vegetable stock

1 chorizo, sliced

2 cups brown mushrooms, cleaned and sliced 2 cloves garlic, finely chopped

1/2 teaspoon fresh ginger, ground 1 long red chili, minced

1/4 cup dry white wine

1/2 cup tomato sauce

1 teaspoon smoked paprika

Kosher salt and ground black pepper, to taste 1 cup green beans

Directions

In a medium saucepan, bring the water to a boil. Add the rice and vegetable stock cube. Stir and reduce the heat. Cover and let it simmer for 20 minutes.

Then, place the chorizo, mushrooms, garlic, ginger, and red chili in the baking pan. Cook at 380 degrees F for 6 minutes, stirring periodically.

Add the prepared rice to the casserole dish. Add the remaining Ingredients and gently stir to combine.

Cook for 6 minutes, checking periodically to ensure even cooking. Serve in individual bowls and enjoy!

Polenta Fries with Sriracha Sauce

(Ready in about 45 minutes + chilling time | Servings 3)

Per serving:

247 Calories; 6.5g Fat; 43.8g Carbs; 3.7g Protein; 11.5g Sugars

Ingredients

Polenta Fries:

1 ½ cups water

1 teaspoon sea salt 1/2 cup polenta

1 tablespoon butter, room temperature A pinch of grated nutmeg

1 teaspoon dried Italian herb mix Sriracha Sauce:

1 red jalapeno pepper, minced

1 garlic clove, minced

1 tablespoon cider vinegar 2 tablespoons tomato paste 1 tablespoon honey

Directions

Bring the water and 1 teaspoon sea salt to a boil in a saucepan; slowly and gradually stir in the polenta, whisking continuously until there are no lumps.

Reduce the heat to simmer and cook for 5 to 6 minutes until the polenta starts to thicken. Cover and continue to simmer for 25 minutes or until you have a thick mixture, whisking periodically.

Stir in the butter, nutmeg, and Italian herbs.

Pour your polenta into a parchment-lined rimmed baking tray, spreading the mixture evenly. Cover with plastic wrap; let it stand in your refrigerator for about 2 hours to firm up.

Then, slice the polenta into strips and place them in the greased Air Fryer basket. Cook in the preheated Air Fryer at 395 degrees F for about 11 minutes.

Meanwhile, make the Sriracha sauce by whisking all Ingredients. Serve the warm polenta fries with the Sriracha sauce on the side. Enjoy!

Pretzel Knots with Cumin Seeds

(Ready in about 25 minutes | Servings 6)

Per serving:

121 Calories; 6.5g Fat; 11.1g Carbs; 3.9g Protein; 3.1g Sugars

Ingredients

1 package crescent refrigerator rolls

2 eggs, whisked with 4 tablespoons of water 1 teaspoon cumin seeds

Directions

Roll the dough out into a rectangle. Slice the dough into 6 pieces.

Roll each piece into a log and tie each rope into a knot. Cover and let it rest for 10 minutes.

Brush the top of the pretzel knots with the egg wash; sprinkle with the cumin seeds. Arrange the pretzel knots in the lightly greased Air Fryer basket.

Bake in the preheated Air Fryer at 340 degrees for 7 minutes until golden brown. Bon appétit!

Puff Pastry Meat Strudel

(Ready in about 40 minutes | Servings 8)

Per serving:

356 Calories; 16g Fat; 35.6g Carbs; 16.5g Protein; 1.7g Sugars

Ingredients

1 tablespoon olive oil 1 small onion, chopped 2 garlic cloves, minced 1/3 pound ground beef 1/3 pound ground pork

2 tablespoons tomato puree 2 tablespoons matzo meal

Sea salt and ground black pepper, to taste 1/2 teaspoon cayenne pepper

1/4 teaspoon dried marjoram

2 cans (8-ounces) refrigerated crescent rolls 1 egg, whisked with 1 tablespoon of water 2 tablespoons sesame seeds

1/2 cup marinara sauce 1 cup sour cream

Directions

Heat the oil in a heavy skillet over medium flame. Sauté the onion just until soft and translucent. Add the garlic and sauté for 1 minute more.

Add the ground beef and pork and continue to cook for 3 minutes more or until the meat is no longer pink. Remove from the heat.

Add the tomato puree and matzo meal.

Roll out the puff pastry and spread the meat mixture lengthwise on the dough. Sprinkle with salt, black pepper, cayenne pepper, and marjoram.

Fold in the sides of the dough over the meat mixture. Pinch the edges to seal.

Place the strudel on the parchment lined Air Fryer basket. Brush the strudel with the egg wash; sprinkle with sesame seeds.

Bake in the preheated Air Fryer at 330 degrees F for 18 to 20 minutes or until the pastry is puffed and golden and the filling is thoroughly cooked.

Allow your strudel to rest for 5 to 10 minutes before cutting and serving. Serve with the marinara sauce and sour cream on the side. Bon appétit!

Rich Couscous Salad with Goat Cheese

(Ready in about 45 minutes | Servings 4)

Per serving:

258 Calories; 13g Fat; 28.3g Carbs; 8.8g Protein; 8.2g Sugars

Ingredients

1/2 cup couscous

4 teaspoons olive oil

1/2 lemon, juiced, zested 1 tablespoon honey

Sea salt and freshly ground black pepper, to your liking 2 tomatoes, sliced

1 red onion, thinly sliced

1/2 English cucumber, thinly sliced 2 ounces goat cheese, crumbled

1 teaspoon ghee

2 tablespoons pine nuts

1/2 cup loosely packed Italian parsley, finely chopped

Directions

Put the couscous in a bowl; now, pour the boiling water over it. Cover and set aside for 5 to 8 minutes; fluff with a fork.

Place the couscous in a cake pan. Transfer the pan to the Air Fryer basket and cook at 360 digress F about 20 minutes. Make sure to stir every 5 minutes to ensure even cooking.

Meanwhile, in a small mixing bowl, whisk the olive oil, lemon juice and zest, honey, salt, and black pepper. Toss the couscous with this dressing.

Add the tomatoes, red onion, English cucumber, and goat cheese; gently stir to combine.

Rub the ghee in the pine nuts, using your hands and place them in the Air Fryer basket. Roast for 4 minutes; give the nuts a good toss. Put the cooking basket back again and roast for a further 3 to 4 minutes.

Scatter the toasted nuts over your salad and garnish with parsley. Enjoy!

Risotto Balls with Bacon and Corn

(Ready in about 30 minutes + chilling time | Servings 6)

Per serving:

435 Calories; 15.6g Fat; 47.4g Carbs; 23.3g Protein; 4.1g Sugars

Ingredients

4 slices Canadian bacon 1 tablespoon olive oil

1/2 medium-sized leek, chopped

1 teaspoon fresh garlic, minced

Sea salt and freshly ground pepper, to taste 1 cup white rice

4 cups vegetable broth 1/3 cup dry white wine

2 tablespoons tamari sauce

1 tablespoon oyster sauce 1 tablespoon butter

1 cup sweet corn kernels

1 bell pepper, seeded and chopped 2 eggs lightly beaten

1 cup bread crumbs

1 cup parmesan cheese, preferably freshly grated

Directions

Cook the Canadian bacon in a nonstick skillet over medium-high heat. Let it cool, finely chop and reserve.

Heat the olive oil in a saucepan over medium heat. Now, sauté the leeks and garlic, stirring occasionally, about 5 minutes. Add the salt and pepper.

Stir in the white rice. Continue to cook approximately 3 minutes or until translucent. Add the warm broth, wine, tamari sauce, and oyster sauce; cook until the liquid is absorbed.

Remove the saucepan from the heat; stir in the butter, corn, bell pepper, and reserved Canadian bacon. Let it cool completely. Then, shape the mixture into small balls.

In a shallow bowl, combine the eggs with the breadcrumbs and parmesan cheese. Dip each ball in the eggs/crumb mixture.

Cook in the preheated Air Fryer at 395 degrees F for 10 to 12 minutes, shaking the basket periodically. Serve warm.

Savory Cheese and Herb Biscuits

(Ready in about 30 minutes | Servings 3)

Per serving:

382 Calories; 22.1g Fat; 35.6g Carbs; 10.3g Protein; 3.1g Sugars

Ingredients

1 cup self-rising flour

1/2 teaspoon baking powder 1/2 teaspoon honey

1/2 stick butter, melted

1/2 cup Colby cheese, grated 1/2 cup buttermilk

1/4 teaspoon kosher salt 1 teaspoon dried parsley

1 teaspoon dried rosemary

Directions

Preheat your Air Fryer to 360 degrees F. Line the cooking basket with a piece of parchment paper.

In a mixing bowl, thoroughly combine the flour, baking powder, honey, and butter. Gradually stir in the remaining Ingredients.

Bake in the preheated Air Fryer for 15 minutes.

Work in batches. Serve at room temperature. Bon appétit!

Smoked Salmon and Rice Rollups

(Ready in about 25 minutes | Servings 3)

Per serving:

226 Calories; 11.6g Fat; 15.1g Carbs; 15.2g Protein; 1.9g Sugars

Ingredients

1 tablespoon fresh lemon juice 6 slices smoked salmon

1 tablespoon extra-virgin olive oil

1/2 cup cooked rice

1 tablespoon whole-grain mustard 3 tablespoons shallots, chopped

1 garlic clove, minced

1 teaspoon capers, rinsed and chopped Sea salt and ground black pepper, to taste 3 ounces sour cream

Directions

Drizzle the lemon juice all over the smoked salmon.

Then, spread each salmon strip with olive oil. In a mixing bowl, thoroughly combine the cooked rice, mustard, shallots, garlic, and capers.

Spread the rice mixture over the olive oil. Roll the slices into individual rollups and secure with a toothpick. Season with salt and black pepper.

Place in the lightly greased Air Fryer basket. Bake at 370 degrees F for 16 minutes, turning them over halfway through the cooking time. Serve with sour cream and enjoy!

Spicy Seafood Risotto

(Ready in about 25 minutes | Servings 3)

Per serving:

445 Calories; 17.7g Fat; 48.8g Carbs; 24.4g Protein; 2.5g Sugars

Ingredients

1 ½ cups cooked rice, cold

3 tablespoons shallots, minced 2 garlic cloves, minced

1 tablespoon oyster sauce

2 tablespoons dry white wine 2 tablespoons sesame oil

Salt and ground black pepper, to taste 2 eggs

4 ounces lump crab meat

1 teaspoon ancho chili powder

2 tablespoons fresh parsley, roughly chopped

Directions

Mix the cold rice, shallots, garlic, oyster sauce, dry white wine, sesame oil, salt, and black pepper in a lightly greased baking pan. Stir in the whisked eggs.

Cook in the preheated Air Fryer at 370 degrees for 13 to 16 minutes.

Add the crab and ancho chili powder to the baking dish; stir until everything is well combined. Cook for 6 minutes more.

Serve at room temperature, garnished with fresh parsley. Bon appétit!

Sunday Glazed Cinnamon Rolls

(Ready in about 15 minutes | Servings 4)

Per serving:

313 Calories; 10.8g Fat; 52.9g Carbs; 2.1g Protein; 39.4g Sugars

Ingredients

1 can cinnamon rolls 2 tablespoons butter

1 cup powdered sugar

1 teaspoon vanilla extract 3 tablespoons hot water

Directions

Place the cinnamon rolls in the Air Fryer basket.

Bake at 300 degrees F for 10 minutes, flipping them halfway through the cooking time.

Meanwhile, mix the butter, sugar, and vanilla. Pour in water, 1 tablespoon at a time, until the glaze reaches desired consistency.

Spread over the slightly cooled cinnamon rolls. Bon appétit!

Sun-Dried Tomato and Herb Pull-Apart Bread

(Ready in about 20 minutes | Servings 6)

Per serving:

412 Calories; 24.4g Fat; 39.1g Carbs; 7.2g Protein; 7g Sugars

Ingredients

1 (16-ounce) can refrigerated buttermilk biscuits 1/2 cup stick butter, melted

1/3 cup parmesan cheese, grated

1/4 cup sun-dried tomatoes 1 teaspoon rosemary

1 teaspoon basil

1 teaspoon oregano 1/2 teaspoon sage 1 teaspoon parsley

2 garlic cloves very finely minced

Directions

Separate your dough into the biscuits and cut each of them in half; roll them into balls. Dip each ball into the butter and begin layering in a nonstick Bundt pan.

Cover the bottom of the pan with one layer of dough balls; then, top the dough balls with half of the cheese and half of the sun-dried tomatoes. Repeat for another layer.

In a small mixing bowl, thoroughly combine the garlic with herbs.

Finish with a third layer of dough and top it with the herb/garlic mixture.

Cook the pull-apart bread in the Air Fryer at 320 degrees for 13 to 16 minutes. Bon appétit!

Taco Stuffed Bread

(Ready in about 15 minutes | Servings 4)

Per serving:

472 Calories; 21.9g Fat; 37.6g Carbs; 30.5g Protein; 6.6g Sugars

Ingredients

1 loaf French bread 1/2 pound ground beef 1 onion, chopped

1 teaspoon garlic, minced 1 package taco seasoning

1 ½ cups Queso Panela, sliced

Salt and ground black pepper, to taste 3 tablespoons tomato paste

2 tablespoons fresh cilantro leaves, chopped

Directions

Cut the top off of the loaf of bread; remove some of the bread from the middle creating a well and reserve.

In a large skillet, cook the ground beef with the onion and garlic until the beef is no longer pink and the onion is translucent.

Add the taco seasoning, cheese, salt, black pepper, and tomato paste. Place the taco mixture into your bread.

Bake in the preheated Air Fryer at 380 degrees F for 5 minutes. Garnish with fresh cilantro leaves. Enjoy!

The Best Fish Tacos Ever

(Ready in about 25 minutes | Servings 3)

Per serving:

493 Calories; 19.2g Fat; 48.4g Carbs; 30.8g Protein; 5.8g Sugars

Ingredients

1 tablespoon mayonnaise 1 teaspoon Dijon mustard 1 tablespoon sour cream

1/2 teaspoon fresh garlic, minced 1/4 teaspoon red pepper flakes Sea salt, to taste

2 bell peppers, seeded and sliced 1 shallot, thinly sliced

1 egg

1 tablespoon water

1 tablespoon taco seasoning mix 1/3 cup tortilla chips, crushed 1/4 cup parmesan cheese, grated

1 halibut fillets, cut into 1-inch strips 6 mini flour taco shells

6 lime wedges, for serving

Directions

Thoroughly combine the mayonnaise, mustard, sour cream, garlic, red pepper flakes, and salt. Add the bell peppers and shallots; toss to coat well. Place in your refrigerator until ready to serve.

Line the Air Fryer basket with a piece of parchment paper.

In a shallow bowl, mix the egg, water, and taco seasoning mix. In a separate shallow bowl, mix the crushed tortilla chips and parmesan.

Dip the fish into the egg mixture, then coat with the parmesan mixture, pressing to adhere.

Bake in the preheated Air Fryer at 380 degrees F for 13 minutes, flipping halfway through the cooking time.

Divide the creamed pepper mixture among the taco shells. Top with the fish, and serve with lime wedges. Enjoy!

Traditional Japanese Onigiri

(Ready in about 30 minutes | Servings 3)

Per serving:

374 Calories; 11.5g Fat; 53.2g Carbs; 12.2g Protein; 1.9g Sugars

Ingredients

3 cups water

1 cup white Japanese rice 1 teaspoon dashi granules 1 egg, beaten

1/2 cup cheddar cheese, grated 1/2 teaspoon kinako

1 tablespoon fish sauce

1/2 teaspoon coriander seeds 1/2 teaspoon cumin seeds

1 teaspoon sesame oil 1/4 cup shallots, chopped Sea salt, to taste

Directions

Bring the vegetable broth to a boil in a saucepan over medium-high heat. Stir in the rice and reduce the heat to simmer; cook about 20 minutes and fluff with a fork.

Mix the cooked rice with the remaining Ingredients and stir until everything is well incorporated.

Then, shape and press the mixture into triangle-shape cakes.

Bake the rice cakes in the preheated Air Fryer at 350 degrees F for about 10 minutes, turning them over halfway through the cooking time.

Serve with seasoned nori, if desired. Bon appétit!

Alphabetical Index

I

CPSIA information can be obtained
at www.ICGtesting.com
Printed in the USA
LVHW081201270521
688664LV00006B/655